War Against the Federal Government!

War Against the People!
War Against One Another!

Gerald Marcus Savage

authorHOUSE®

AuthorHouse™
1663 Liberty Drive
Bloomington, IN 47403
www.authorhouse.com
Phone: 833-262-8899

Published by AuthorHouse 07/22/2020

ISBN: 978-1-4520-8008-6 (sc)
ISBN: 978-1-4520-8009-3 (e)

Library of Congress Control Number: 2011900839

Print information available on the last page.

This book is printed on acid-free paper.

About the Author

The author is a 40 year old ex-logger and mechanic from the hills of North Mississippi who is currently retired broke? He is hoping to retain the American Dream once again in the future if that is at all possible.

About the Book

I'm writing this book in the hopes that people everywhere of all races, political groups, and religions will see and realize that our constitution and capitalist system are being destroyed and that if we (the America People) don't wake up and stand up for what's right then our country will soon be lost.

Free Preview

If you were going to choose between the people who founded this country (the forefathers), and those who are running it today, who would you choose to stand with? In this book I discuss just a few of the many issues which are dividing our country today. I talk about how there is an assault on our constitution, capitalist system, and religious institutions. How we're losing our freedoms. How our way of life is being changed, and not for the better. How we as a people have strayed from our founding principles and how now our country has an important choice in history to make; a choice which will decide the fate of America forever!

Patriot Act

Cap & Trade

Health Care

Unconstitutional laws

Religious and moral divide

Racial divide

Political divide

↓

↓

Leads to
Anarchy → → → WAR!!

I think the ones in power are the tyrants and the patriots are the terrorists.

G.S.

I came up with the idea for this book sitting at home sick, unemployed, and living on government subsidies; which I don't agree with. I have been waiting years for things to get better in this country, for freedom to come back, and for a few more people to speak out on this issue. Well, I can't take waiting anymore.

I see my country being destroyed, and I won't sit by idle anymore while it happens. I must speak my mind and relieve some of the thoughts that I have about freedom, laws, and the constitution which have built up over the years. We are on the verge of economic collapse, civil and world war.

Evidently, I am among the few people (crazy) who see where we are headed as a country. It is not hard to see the future if you study a little science, history, the Bible or Bibles; as I am intrigued by people of all faiths, and try to understand God, and the people of today and yesterday.

Who am I? I'm just a pot smoker from the hills of

Mississippi, who loves his country and hates injustice. Oh yeah, I am also a manic-depressive in an elated state of mind, so be ready for anything.

There are so many things I see wrong in our country today, so I am going to try and touch on a few of them that I can think of at the moment. Where to start, well I guess we can start with a few questions, since my book will have more questions than answers.

If you were going to choose between the people who founded this country (the Forefathers) and those who are running it today, who would you choose to stand with? We know and have known that we have gotten away from the founding principles, one of the most important to me small and limited government.

We also know that our constitution is being shredded and if people do not wake up and stand up then freedom and the American way of life as we know it will be totally gone, and When America is gone, so will go the freedom of the rest of the world.

Our constitution is a sacred document like the Bible, because it also was inspired by God and written by man. Many in the country today would say that our constitution is a living document subject to changes as a living being would be, or that it should even be done away with entirely, along with every right it guarantees.

These people would say we are more modern today

and need new ideas, and that the old ideas (Constitution including the Bill of Rights) are out dated and should be done away with, and replaced with new and more progressive ideas. For instance, people would say that the "Right to Bear Arms" applied only during more primitive times when our nation did not have a military. That when the constitution was written the individual had to police and protect themselves, and that today we have modern police forces to protect us. These facts are true. We have a military and we have police, but there is also another reason equally important to the forefathers in the right to bear arms, and that was so the people could protect themselves from a corrupt government.

The Forefathers had just come from and were fighting a corrupt government. This was a government that before the revolutionary war had tried its best to keep guns and especially machine technology out of the hands of the colonists.

After the revolutionary war George Washington and the other founding fathers had a choice to make, stay the course for freedom or do whatever they wanted, since they were running the country now. Thank God they were Godly men who were not greedy or evil and that they stayed the course of freedom and rule by the people.

George Washington could have set himself up as dictator, but he declined as well as the other forefathers.

They just wanted to be free. It had been a long hard War, and George himself just wanted to go home to Mount Vernon and go back to making whiskey and running his plantation, but he stayed on for a couple of terms longer for the sake of the country and his fellow man. Would any of today's leaders have done the same and let the people keep the power? What would you have done?

Thomas Jefferson and many others at the time knew the only way to keep the country free and ruled by the people was to let the people keep the right to bear arms, an essential part of a truly free nation.

A quote by Thomas Jefferson states,

"The tree of liberty must be refreshed from time to time with the blood of patriots and tyrants!"

Now let's move on up in time to the period just before the American Civil War. During this time the country was just as it is today strongly divided on many hot issues. Slavery was not the only issue, nor was it the main issue. It was about the economy and right and wrong. In 1860 when Abraham Lincoln was elected president, without the Southern vote, the South had had enough!

What do you do when you have exhausted all your remedies? When evil, in your mind, has taken over your country? Not much if you are a Fascist, Marxist, Socialist, Communist, or ruled by an evil dictator, but if you are a free people with the "Right to Bear Arms" and have a constitution protecting you and your rights then you separate yourselves, or succeed. That is just what the South did, and you need to understand who these people were during this time period. They were direct family and friends of the Forefathers, people who knew or had known the Forefathers and enemies to them or people who opposed their ideals.

People separated themselves but eventually division, as it almost always does, lead to war and much bloodshed. History says the North won the war and the South lost; however, as a country I would say both sides won, because freedom won as a whole. If that war had not taken place, had not been fought, then I think our rights and constitution would have been gone a long time ago.

The Forefathers set up our government this way so the people could fight and keep their rights and freedoms if ever threatened by corrupt government. This very concept is one of the reasons why Mr. Robert E. Lee, Jefferson Davis, and many other Confederate Soldiers were spared after the Civil War instead of being put to death. They had a fundamental right to do what they did. Our constitution gives us these rights.

From the time of the Civil War until present day America has been through a great deal. We know all too well that a country is only as good as its leaders.

Good and evil, opposing one another constantly, but what has happened to our country these days? Is evil in the majority? It seems to be, otherwise why would our so called leaders destroy our country as they have been doing? Do they not realize they are destroying themselves, their own friends, and family? Do they even care, or is it all about money and material gain for them? How can it be that so few people seem to have any common sense these days?

Let's start with the Mexican Border, an old problem promised to be fixed decades ago. Remember President Ronald Reagan, he granted amnesty back in 1986. However, the border still was not sealed. Again today, amnesty is being considered. But granting amnesty without sealing and securing the border first would be like someone pouring grain into a giant grain bin with an enormous hole where the grain is spilling onto the ground and trying to pick up the grain off the ground, while steadily pouring in more. Insanity!

We all know the border must be sealed first, so why isn't the Federal Government doing its job? Why won't the Federal Government seal its own border? I have wondered this for years, but especially since 9/11. The government says terrorists are going to kill us. We know spies, thugs, outlaws, and major drug dealers are in our country; so what is the deal? I could get a bunch of these old hill boys from the South, with their shotguns and seal it, so why can't or won't the Federal Government do the same.

I say put a military sniper every half mile or so along the border. Create a gun line and let people have no misconception about what happens if they cross that line. Not only on the Mexican border but the Canadian Border, also. Once this is done amnesty for immigrants already here would be fine. This would be money well spent. Would you not protect your home from invasion, then why not your country?

Another good thing would be to help Mexico with their drug wars then the Mexican Government would be able to help us. We should all be helping each other, except I wonder if our government is not as corrupt as Mexico's government, just better at concealing it.

Another issue is if the Federal Government won't seal the border, then why won't they let the states do it? Maybe the Federal government or certain people influencing the government have certain interests in leaving the border open. After all a great deal of drugs, guns, and money do cross our Southern Border. How deep might our government's corruption go and how much more deadlock can our country stand?

Why would the Federal government sue a state, any state, over anything, especially an issue which it has control over and declines to fix? The Federal Government by law is supposed to control the borders;

therefore, it is the Federal Governments responsibility to resolve the border control issue. If your neighbor sued you over something crazy would things ever be the same in your neighborhood? Will things ever be the same in this country again in our lifetime?

The Federal Government is made up of, "the people, for the people, by the people." You and I are the government and the Federal government is composed of our friends and neighbors, so let me ask you again, what would you do or how would you feel if your neighbor sued you? So now we can say the Federal government is composed of our friends, neighbors, and enemies.

Speaking of suing, it is an issue in itself. Suing for money was something unheard of at the start of our country. One reason why that was, I think, was because of the practice of dueling. Dueling was a practice that had been around for hundreds of years. Dueling was nothing more than calling an opponent out for a fair fight with equal weapons. Dueling did not mean someone had to die, or even be hurt, although it did mean death sometimes.

Our seventh president Andrew Jackson was a duelist as were many other prominent politicians and people of the times. Alexander Hamilton and Aaron Burr are other prime examples. Dueling stopped the need for frivolous lawsuits, because it usually settled any matter or argument on the spot.

I am not saying bring back dueling, although that would be fine with me, but frivolous lawsuits are one of the main reasons why our insurances and everything else are so high in America today. Suing for excessive amounts of money is wrong and should be virtually ban. If you have wronged someone then you should have to pay, within reason, the value of the damages. I don't, however, feel that a person should have to pay tens or hundreds of times the damage, usually going to lawyers who help make the law this way for their own benefit.

Suing screws up our economy, and an economy is the most important part of a nation. Our enemies around the world know and understand this concept. That is the reason why on 9-11 our Trade Centers were hit, not to kill Americans, but to kill the American Economy. You can have a mighty economy without a mighty military, but you cannot have a mighty military without a mighty economy. Also you can build a mighty military over night with a good economy or if you have a good industrial base (WWII), but with a poor economy and little or no industrial base left here in the United States we cannot build anything. We are defeated economically and then militarily, we just don't know it yet. Also when the towers were hit we were drawn, by poor leadership into the situation we are currently in overseas, which is working in the favor of our enemies because these wars are breaking our economy and dividing us and our military. Whoever our enemies are and I believe a lot of them to be here in the United States, they are pretty smart, smarter than a lot of our leaders in Washington, for sure.

The money we are wasting on these wars could be used for infrastructure, science, research and development, and the development of America's welfare in general (not welfare system). We need to be helping the sick and homeless people by getting good Americans back working so they can help solve some of these problems in their own towns and neighborhoods.

We need to get rid of the Federal income tax. We know this tax was started at the beginning of the last civil war, and it should be abolished like slavery. Our whole tax system is corrupt and needs simplifying. I am for basically one flat tax. If God only asked for ten percent once, then how can man ask for ten percent, ten times?

Work is another thing, and it shouldn't be penalized but instead rewarded, and no business is ever too big to fail. Best we all fall together, least we fall apart. I look at the bailouts like a game of Monopoly. If your opponents in the game are going to cheat and steal from the bank then we, as honest players in the game, can never win. We can never progress any further as long as this insanity in the game goes on. So what do we do? Do we quit and accept defeat, or do we turn the table over and fight? (Lots of Conspiracies) The bailouts were unconstitutional and hurt our capitalist system even more, only postponing the inevitable and making things worse in the end.

If we were bankrupt we should have just declared bankruptcy as a country and started over as an individual would do. Now after borrowing and blowing all this money maybe we can get it right, and declare bankruptcy twice the next time when the economy collapses again. The sad thing about all of it, we the American people didn't get anything much out of the trillions spent or stolen, except a debt.

Cutting taxes, curbing government waste, and spending would help a lot of things. Competition in the market place is also an answer to many problems. Competition with each other and not the Federal Government! The bailouts were wrong and they killed competition. They gave the ones on top all the money and control. The middle class and the little man have little hope. He can no longer compete in the market place. What does he do? Get out of the game? I hope not, because to get out of this game means death and death is no game.

A country is just like an individual. It cannot spend what it does not have, or should not. Only a strong fiscal house can stand. You cannot help others if you cannot help yourself. Just about everything our government is doing right now is destroying us. I don't believe an evil dictator who hates us could do a better job.

We need to be getting our industrial base back here in America. We need to be self sufficient as a country. An industrial base is needed and is essential to every aspect of our security, not just economic. I was talking with a good friend of mine, who is a machinist. We were discussing the fact that during World War II our industrial base was here at home, and was converted to making war materials and weapons to defend the country. Examples of well known factories that made this conversion include Ford and General Motors.

We talked about what happens if our government keeps sending all our factories overseas and putting industrial companies out of business. We not only lose jobs and job security, but we also lose the ability to defend our country in the event of a major world war and invasion by a foreign power. We lose all security.

A military is no good without equipment and weapons. The fact is that with fewer machine tools and machines in the country to work with, we will have to make and build more, and while we are making tools and building machines, our enemy will be making and building weapons, a scary thought, but true.

Talking about war makes me think of the military. The majority of these men and women are some of the best in the country, and they deserve some sweat and blood back from the rest of us. They have been on a mission they have had no control over. They have been lied to by Democrats and Republicans alike. The Democrats said they would bring them home and then Obama sent tens of thousands of more troops overseas after he took office. Our military is stretched and stressed out. Many of our service men and women have lost their families, homes, friends, body parts, and lives; for what? We need to bring our soldiers home and serve and protect them for awhile. Make them comfortable and let them relax.

Our country is in pain. It needs to heal and cannot as long as the war goes on. Can anyone out there hear me? Does anyone care or think of anyone but themselves, or anything but material gain? We are going to really need our military one day in the near future, if not for the threat of invasion and world war, then civil unrest, because our country is headed toward economic collapse, anarchy, and ruin. What worries me are all the divisions in our country today; division of race, division of religion, division in politics, and division of principles.

The reason America is going down is because of the same things that make it great including diverse races and religions. However, the concept of diversity is working against us today. In decades past our country was run by a mostly white Christian, all male majority.

This means they generally could all agree on a few things from time to time, unlike today where we have all races, religions, sexual orientations, etc; who don't agree on anything and now we have a real mess.

I am not saying we need all white male Christians in our government. I would not care if our leaders were all black, Asian, women, Muslims, or whatever; just as long as they can agree sometime about what is right and are good leaders. However; the odds of this body of diverse people in our government getting together for what is right for our country seems unlikely.

Other divisions in our country are our vast differences in state laws. It is like going from one country to another every time you cross a state line. I'll give you a couple of examples. I know a man who is serving 30 years in prison here in Mississippi on a marijuana charge, while some states up North and out West have legalized cannabis for medical use and California is voting on legalizing the substance all the way and taxing it. Currently, it is being smoked, cultivated, and traded with ease in many states in the country. In fact, The University of Mississippi has the Nation's only legalized marijuana farm and has been growing pot for the government since the 1970's for research. However, Mississippi still doesn't have legalized marijuana for medical use. How long will it be, if ever, before it is legal in Mississippi?

If Mississippi does legalize marijuana will the laws

be retroactive and let people like the man I am talking about out of prison, or will he have to serve the whole 30 year sentence simply because of state lines, geography, and differences in law. If we are all Americans then why aren't our laws a little more uniform?

Why don't we all have to suffer the same injustices? Why is it that some Americans are free to choose on certain issues; good or bad, while other Americans never get that choice? If we are all equally free then why don't we all feel like it? Again, why aren't our laws more uniform? Example two of the many divisions of our country when it comes to the states and state laws is our Second Amendment Right to keep and bear arms. Why it is legal in some states or places to have a gun while in other places or states it is illegal? If we are all Americans with guaranteed constitutional rights, then how can those rights end at a state or city line when we are still in America and still Americans? Your Second Amendment Rights should apply to the Country as a whole, and I mean the whole country. You should be able to cross any line, anywhere, anytime, and still be legal to carry a gun if you were legal to start with. However, we know that is not true.

Oh, I understand states rights, one of the greatest principles in our constitution, but I do not think the Forefathers meant for us to be quite so diverse, or divided as we are today when it comes to our freedom, rights, or laws. The Forefathers just wanted to be free, but I don't have a choice.

Just like the seatbelt laws, these are good laws for babies, kids, or anyone under the age of 21, but adults should have the right to choose (Oh, I forgot, insurance lobbyists and Big Business). I have had friends who have wrecked vehicles, as I have myself, where they definitely would have been killed and I probably would have come out worse wearing a seatbelt myself. There is the thing of being paralyzed also, and on the other side of the argument seatbelts have saved a lot of people by keeping them from being thrown from the car, but also people have been burned alive, because they could not get out of their seatbelts. It is a life issue like abortion. Abortionists have the right to choose life or death for their baby, so why can't we choose life or death for ourselves? This is a right God has given to us all, but man has taken this right away. According to our constitution and my understanding of it and the Forefathers these laws are unconstitutional.

You are riding your motorcycle in one state legally with no helmet when you cross a state line, or as I say state border, and now you no longer are free to choose if you wear a motorcycle helmet or not. You can be fined or jailed for not wearing it. Again, it is a life issue, but your personal life and choice, choosing for yourself. Not like abortion where the mother or someone else chooses for the baby, and then the baby must accept it, because it is the baby, and the baby's rights that don't matter. I said it, from birth till death your rights don't matter anymore in the United States.

Now lets us talk a little about politics. Money must be taken out of our political system. There is too much money changing hands during our election process, and once in office through lobbyists. Laws must be made to stop this evil in our political system. Lawmakers should be going by what is right, what helps our country, and not by who pays them the most money or gives them the best gifts.

Speaking of gifts our lawmakers or congress could use the gift of term limits.

Another thing that is alarming to me is how some politicians do not write their own speeches and do not even know what they are talking about if they lose their written speech. Leaders who cannot write their own speeches or do not understand the issues themselves are not leaders. If you listen to a politician whose speech is written by someone else, and you like what you hear, then you should vote for the speech writer and not that candidate or politician. If a man cannot talk without someone else telling him what to say, what good is he and is he a leader? A leader cannot be picked or made by man, but is born to lead and must be found. Just like a general who is a leader who used to lead from the front

,but these days the leader or general may be giving orders over the phone from behind the lines or somewhere else, so is this a leader? A leader needs to be out front, otherwise how can we follow?

Health care is another big issue for our country. I could write on the subject for hours, but I will only make one quick point and move on. I think all health care is doing is unionizing the country. I mean think about it, the unions already pretty much have top notch government approved health care, so basically all they are doing is turning over their insurance responsibilities to the government who forces all other non-union businesses to get equal coverage. In a sense this unionizes or socializes them all because before long all the private insurers will all be gone, because private business cannot compete with the government. Heath care will further put us into bankruptcy and financial ruin.

The United States energy policy is another issue and would take hours to discuss. I will touch on one quick point that is most important to me. Oil is a necessary part of our lives and we must have it to survive economically. Not drilling for oil today would be like lawmakers stopping horse breeding in the 1800's, doing away with horses, before we even had the idea for the combustible engine running in the car. In other words, you do not get rid of what works before you have something better to replace it.

Our government should be drilling for oil and natural gas at the rate we are going to war overseas. Supply and demand: the more oil we have the cheaper it will be. Also, the stronger and more secure our economy will be. The high price of oil is one of the main things that killed our economy right before Bush left office. Inflation will come back or there will be a major war in the Middle East and the price of oil will go up again, taking down our economy for the final count, and us with it.

Now let's talk a little about outlaws and crooks. People who break mans laws are outlaws. People who break Gods laws are sinners. People who break both man and Gods laws are crooks. Outlaws and crooks are both sinners, because God said to live by his laws, but also to respect and do your best to uphold man's laws. However, man has made laws now, more than ever, that are just unconstitutional. Unconstitutional laws or unjust laws cause the people who are law abiding citizens and are caught up by these laws to be turned into outlaws. (Health Care, Cap-n-Trade)

An example of a crook would be a politician who lies and makes laws that are unjust for the purpose of advancing his or her agenda or those of lobbyists. The politician has lied (stolen the truth) therefore, breaking

Gods law, and made a law which is unconstitutional, which breaks both man and Gods law.

An example of an outlaw would be someone who does not wear their helmet, or seatbelt, or smokes pot (Willie Nelson).

Since pot is natural and created or allowed to be here by God then man should not outlaw it. Outlawing things like this only creates a black-market controlled by crooks. Outlaws are usually killed or go to jail when caught breaking the law, while crooks (politicians who break the law) are given little if any punishment. This is not right and needs to be changed.

A politician, deputy sheriff, police officer, mayor or anyone in a position of power, usually wealthy, who has great authority, should suffer strong consequences when caught in an act of corruption. With their money and power they can influence, corrupt, or hurt more innocent people. Politicians and lawmakers should be the supreme example of the rule of law.

Gods laws -10 Commandments

God and mans laws- Constitution

Unconstitutional laws- Devil (Evil)

Now we come to some of the problems with our

economy. Since the government is taking over everything (illegally) and hiring tens of thousands of government workers to oversee us, the American people, then why don't they start some government programs to put the American people back to work until things get better?

Jobs like we had during the 1930's depression. Programs which would educate, invigorate, and help people survive these hard times. These employees could be hired to upgrade our infrastructure and all the other things that have been neglected and are falling apart in our country. The programs of the 1930's may not have been capitalist in nature, but were good and necessary at the time. While what the government is doing today, with too big to fail, by bailing out or buying up private businesses is socialization. This is wrong, because capitalism is the only form of government that works with our constitution. When capitalism is gone so will go the constitution and all our freedoms.

The reason I call myself a constitutional capitalist

Free Market- capitalism

Free people- constitution

In order to be a free people we must have a free market.

If we had the freedom of the Forefathers and combined it with the knowledge and technology of today, there is no limit to what we could accomplish as a people. We have to have a free market to succeed. I understand that there is certain regulation that is good and needed, but over regulation restricts the free market. Over regulation can be just as bad as or even worse than taxes on an economy.

We have not changed as a people since the last great depression, except for the fact that our knowledge and technology are far greater. We still have the same strong intelligent people. We still have just as many resources and materials and even better ways to get to them and use them, so what is the problem? The government is standing in the way with too many regulations and too many taxes. I say it again and again and when we are taxed too much it takes our freedom, because your money is your freedom.

Religion is another issue and is something that can be tricky to talk about for many people. All religions believe in the same thing or should, God and the betterment of man. If this is the case then why all the division, hate, and hypocrisy

People say Bush was the antichrist, Obama is the antichrist, and so on; well anyone in power who is taking our country in the direction we are currently headed is in my opinion the antichrist in the sense we all have good and evil in us, and now we are allowing that evil to get the best of us and our world.

It is the job of the churches; not the government, to take care of the homeless, the sick, the needy, and the downtrodden; so where are the majority of these churches of all religions? Looks to me like our churches are failing us all and we are all failing God.

What does Christianity say about turning the other cheek, Christians? We should ask that our enemies become our friends and we should try to seek peace and work together for the betterment of the world and us all. Where is the voice of the churches and religions as a whole? Do not all religions have moral values and respect for each other? Let us look at abortion. Abortion should be allowed only in cases of incest, rape, or health problems to the mother, but not in any other circumstances. Young women and men both should be more educated and more responsible not be like the too big to fail, bailed out, but instead responsible for their own deeds.

Moral values are the cornerstone of any successful country. Even if there was no God, moral values are required for a nation to exist. Take Rome as an example, war and loss of moral values along with economic decline destroyed Rome. This brings me to homosexuality, gender change or transgender, gay marriage, and so on which are all immoral. I say so because God says so in the Bibles of most all people and religions in this country and the world. These have been the teachings for thousands of years. When as a people are we going to come together for what is right? All individuals of all races and religions should become one in our faith for the common good of all. We should come together to believe in one God with many ways to obtain God, through our faiths, being non-hypocritical of each other and letting God judge.

I heard Obama talking before he became president in a speech on religion and public policy about how we should all give up or compromise our faith in order for all religions to come together as one. He did not say put aside religion as I do, but to put aside our faith which is God. I will not compromise my God, my country, my family, or my friends for any person or reason even if it means torture or death. I do not expect anyone else to either no matter what race or religion they may be.

It is not about Democrat or Republican, Muslim or Christian, black or white. It is not about politics, race, religion, or creed. It is about the same thing it has been about since the beginning of time, right and wrong. That is the issue we should all focus on. That is where our differences lie.

This brings me to a thought about our constitution.

The reason our constitution is being talked about being changed on so many issues is not because the world is changing, but because people are changing. People are getting further away from God. God said, "I am the same today, tomorrow, and forever." God is good and does not change, so why change our constitution which is good also? If people were more like God they would not be changing as much either.

Now another issue that is very shocking is the new executive order to suspend due process of the law for Americans, and not just those directly on the battlefield. Our president and government have circumvented our constitution and the basic human rights and laws of decency of all men and the world by going around due process and suspending Americans right to trial, right to face your accuser, etc. Just all basic rights that may save you if you are accused of a crime and you are innocent and can prove it. Otherwise, we go straight to the death penalty and who is going to decide who dies and who does not? Who is going to decide without rule of law? Who dies? Who is killed? If it is off the battlefield and not an act of war then how can it be legal to kill an American citizen or anyone else for that matter without a trial?

Speaking of war, what will happen if America breaks up? Once our freedom and power as a nation are in question the rest of the world will fall into civil and world war. North and South Korea will be at war. The Middle East will blow up, while Israel and Iran clash with one another. South America will be in even more turmoil with alliances between Venezuela, Russia, and Iran. The United States Southern Border States will be over run and there will be war on all fronts. It is coming soon if things do not change.

In this book I have discussed just a few of the many issues that are dividing our country today. I have talked about how there is an assault on our constitution, capitalist system, and religious institutions. How we are losing our freedoms. I have discussed how our way of life is being changed, and not for the better. I have also talked about the founding fathers and how our country was founded on God and moral values. How we have strayed from those values and how our country now has an important choice in history to make.

Will we stick with our constitution and all the freedoms it establishes and protects? Will we do away with the free market? Will we throw away everything that every good American has ever fought and died for since the founding of this country?

Will you, as Americans, give up your hope, your faith, your principles, or your dreams? Well I will not give up on my country. I will not give up my faith in God and moral values. I will make concessions on many issues, any issue, but this one and that is where we're headed with todays divison of people and unconstitutional laws. What are we going to do as a nation if we cannot save our country through the election process, or settle our differences through the U.S. court system? What are we going to do when we are asked to compromise our beliefs?

When we see our constitution being shredded, our capitalist system destroyed, every moral value degraded, and our churches broken up? Will we quit the game and give in to evil, or separate ourselves? This is the most important question. If all else fails, what will we do then? Will we give in when it comes to our beliefs or will we stand up and fight for what is right?

We can either come together as one country in unity and save our country from civil war, or we can divide ourselves further in division and prepare ourselves for civil war. If it comes down to it this will not be a war against religion or each other but a war against evil, against division, against greed, against injustice, against ignorance, and all bad things that destroy a nation.

I do not know what anyone else will do, if we cannot come together soon to solve our problems, but me I will not give up on my beliefs. I will not lose my Faith. I will use it on the battlefield against my enemies if it comes down to it. I know everyone has heard the motto, "If you can't beat em, join em." Well my motto is, "If you can't beat em die trying."

Guns and religion are a perfect combination to a successful revolution, also a perfect combination to keeping your freedom if it comes down to it. Right or wrong, good or evil, that is the choice we all have to make. All I can say to people is to follow your own heart, never lose the faith, and pray to God because the time is coming near for the end of our country.

It is better to live for something, than to die for nothing.

It is better to die for something, than to live for nothing.
G.S. 07

This is a newspaper article that I wrote in the early 90's and paid to have printed in my home-town newspaper. I have seen a lot of this coming for a long time.

America

America is a great country full of a lot of great people from all colors, races, and religions. We are still a free country, or so most people say. However, we are losing that freedom every day. Here recently my family and the courts sent me off because they said I had a drinking problem. Even though I am over the age of 21, I was still not allowed to contact my lawyer and have my side of the story heard.

The law came to my house, handcuffed me, and took me to jail. When I asked to call my lawyer for my defense, the law told me that I had no right because I was not under arrest. I was handcuffed and put in jail, but not under arrest. This made me wonder, so I said to myself if I am to get my right to my lawyer then I must make them place me under arrest. When the officer came to get me from my jail cell, I hit him and dropped my hands and said, "Now place me under arrest and give me my right to call my lawyer." Still that right was not given. I was taken into the next room where various legal papers and documents were being read and signed.

Instead of an alcohol/drug abuse center, I heard them discussing a mental hospital. Well, this made me angry and crazy. There was nothing wrong with my mind and I knew it. I kicked the desk and scuffled with the officer. Finally, I calmed down and realized that I was on my way and could only try and make the best of it. It wasn't easy. I have nothing against medical doctors, but doctors that talk about the mind worry me, if you know what I mean.

Well, they kept me drugged up the first day or so, and on what they called, "fifteen minute check." It's a good thing too, because all that was on my mind was escape, and if I would have gotten an opening, I would have taken it. Well about the second day, my cousin and girlfriend came up and this helped me a lot. They calmed me down and convinced me that if I was to ever get out I had to work with the people at the hospital the best I could. That's what I did and after a week, I was released and transferred to St. Dominic's Hospital in Jackson. After a week down there, I was discharged and allowed to come home. It was quite an experience for me. Even though I hated it, I did meet a lot of nice people and managed to learn some good things from my trip. I think if I had been given my right to my lawyer, its one trip that I wouldn't have had to take. I think that many people are sent off every day just as I was because their rights are taken away just as mine were.

Now changing the subject, I think that there are a lot of laws and rights in this country that just aren't right. For example, the equal rights or redistricting laws which say equal. Equal means 50/50 or at least that is what I was taught when I went to school. Well, everybody knows that the blacks in our country receive more than 50% of the voting age. How is this possible? Is there not a contradiction in the law somewhere?

Maybe it is just me and what I was taught in school was wrong, because when I was in school we said the pledge of allegiance to the flag and a prayer to God. Well you know now that prayer and God have been taken out of the schools, and in some parts of the country, the American flag burned-burned on television and laughed at. Just like the Vietnam vets who were spit on and laughed at when they came home from the Vietnam War.

War is another thing: you are a man at 18 and can die for your country, but you're not old enough to do anything else until you're 21.

Everybody wants their rights—gay rights, black

rights, rights, right, etc. This is fine but I think that most rights need to be right only at home on your own land. Gays want it to be taught in school that being gay is right and healthy. Well, I say if I ever have any kids and these laws have been enacted, my kids won't attend American school because they won't be taught that being gay is right. They'll be taught against it.

If gay people can be gay in public and have rights in public, then why can't I smoke a marijuana cigarette on my own land if I want to? Why is the American government buzzing my house every summer and invading my privacy with their helicopters, knocking things off the shelves and walls in my house and in my friends' and neighbor's houses? I think that for this to be America, everyone must have his or her rights, whatever they may be. But I think that these rights should only be right on your own land and that out in public, we must have respect for each other's rights which means queer behavior, smoking pot, or whatever should be done at home, out of town, and out of the general public's eyes.

Another thing that bothers me is the free trade agreement with Mexico. I know Mexico needs help and jobs but to be slave labor is not what they need. The big, rich companies up North are rebasing their companies in Mexico, therefore, American jobs are being lost. This is destroying our economy and isn't helping Mexico that much either. Our government has to make laws to stop this, to make it too costly for American companies to go to Mexico, to make it more profitable for them to stay in America and rebase in America once again, therefore giving hundreds of thousands of Americans their jobs back. If we want to help Mexico, let's give them the technology and knowledge to help themselves in their own country. The North talked about the South in the 1800s for making slaves out of the black people. Well, I ask the people in the government who have made these laws to allow big businesses to move to Mexico: What are you making of the Mexicans except slaves?

These are just a few things that have been on my mind and I thought that before I lose my right to freedom of speech, I would use it. I say to the people wanting to take the flying rights, the hunting & fishing rights the gun rights, that I live by the American flag and I respect the American flag, but if it comes down to it, I will die by the Rebel flag.

Gerald M. Savage
Crazy Man

P.S. Parkwood and St. Dominic hospitals have done wonders for me and as long as nobody messes with my ride, my woman, or my family, I'll be fine.

Wake up America, I love you, or I wouldn't be talking to you. We have to make that choice. Good or evil, that is the question. Evil always has and always will lurk in the darkness, and as good Americans it is our job to shine the light of truth upon that evil, but when evil comes out of the darkness into the open, and people go to defending evil and wrong, then it is our job to fight that wrong with the truth. What is the truth? Well, if you do not know, study your history; don't take my word or anyone else's. Study it for yourself. Truth has no sex, color, race, or religion. It is the truth and never changes. Truth is only principle. Do not only study your history, but the history of others, and other countries and nation's. Study up on how and why our nation was formed and founded. Study the U.S. constitution. Study our capitalist system and how it works with our constitution. Study Marxism, Socialism, and Communism. Study the rise to power of Adolf Hitler in Nazi Germany during World War II with his socialist agenda and the takeover of Europe. See the similarities between then and now. It does not have to be an in-depth study, just a brief study will do. Compare these facts with our world and country today. Study the new health care law and understand how it is nothing more than socialization or socialism. Understand that communism and a dictator will come later or next if we do not stop it.

Socialism- from each according to his ability to each according to his deeds.

Communism- from each according to his ability to each according to his needs.

It may be ten years from now before this happens, and before we see the real damaging effects of all these unconstitutional laws and these illegal presidential executive orders which have been circumventing our constitution. We may have ten years, but I figure much less. We have to stop this socialist, communist takeover of our country from within our government. We have to stop the United Nations and their planned one world socialist order which is coming if we don't stop it.

We must stand together in the truth to do this. Form your own opinion, but with the true facts. We have to make that choice, good or evil without prejudice. The truth is all we have, and only it will save us and keep us free. Study up and make your own decision, America. I have formed my opinion and made my decision. I'll fight for my freedom and the freedom of my family, blood for blood if it comes down to it. God bless you and all who are good and true, but what will you do?

DOWN WITH SOCIALISM AND COMMUNISM IN AMERICA!! DOWN WITH EVIL!!

*Some of the greatest triumphs
throughout history have
come from Failure!*

Waco

Ruby Ridge

Oklahoma City

9-11

Crooks

Bailouts

Moral Values

↓

↓

Succession → →War!!

*The more freedoms a government takes from its
people the more violence there is, the more violence
there is, the more freedoms a government takes,
and so on until it is a police state; or Hell.*